TRANSFORMING TREES

A POETIC EXPLORATION OF TIME HOPE & HUMAN EXISTENCE

AMY CECILIA GRAINGER

TRANSFORMING TREES

AMY CECILIA GRAINGER

©2025 Amy Cecilia Grainger
All rights reserved.

First published 2025

No part of this publication may be reproduced, stored in a retrieval system, or transmitted in any form or by any means—electronic, mechanical, photocopying, recording, or otherwise—without prior written permission of the author.

Disclaimer:
This work reflects the author's philosophical inquiry and lived experience. It is intended for personal reflection and creative exploration only and does not constitute professional advice or instruction. Readers remain solely responsible for their own interpretations and actions.

Author:
Amy Cecilia Grainger

Published by
Souls of Ones Feet

Graphic Design & Cover:
Ged L. M. Buick
ISBN: 978-1-0683830-1-4
:

'When I sit in nature I feel connected to a world beyond our world.'

"When transformation aligns with timelessness
There resides a space to breathe
Love and hope bring harmony
Patience aids to heal"

THE EVER EXPANDING NOW

BEGINNING
In the beginning there was dust, molecules and magic – a dance so extravagantly tragic, a collision, a composure, of a new world that grows older – the beginning – kept expanding – and now – times is not withstanding.

BRIDGE
Welcome to this poetic exploration of time, space, human existence and hope. Feel this book as a gift, a journey of from my heart to yours.

Release any expectations.

Allow yourself to travel – to unravel – to evolve as you explore!

BEACON
Allow the words of these explorations to illuminate the avenues of your time.

Feel love, feel peace, feel hope in your heart.

Be time.

BACK TO A BEGINNING
When we evolve time disintegrates - we uncover a space often reserved or overlooked - time does not end.

It infinitely- begins again.

CONTENT

THE EVER-EXPANDING NOW..........................7
MESSAGE FROM THE AUTHOR 11
INSPIRATION SURROUNDS US 14
THE TREES ETERNAL FLOW...........................19

FLOW ONE 26
FLOW TWO 30
FLOW THREE..................................34
FLOW FOUR...................................38
FLOW FIVE 42
FLOW SIX......................................46

FLOW SEVEN................................50
FLOW EIGHT................................54
FLOW NINE..................................58
FLOW TEN....................................62
FLOW ELEVEN 66
FLOW TWELVE...........................68

POETIC EXTENSION INTRO................75
SEASON OF TIME................................78
MORE IN THIS SERIES.........................81
INVITATION TO EXPLORE FURTHER.............84

"The Souls of One's Feet brings healing
When we connect through this space in time
There is a trajectory held within each of us
A core understanding divine"

MESSAGE FROM THE AUTHOR

HOW DOES IT FEEL TO BE HUMAN?

Welcome to this poetic series, which offers an alternative way to examine a philosophy of hope - a philosophy I refer to as the Souls of One's Feet.

This journey began long before I could grasp the depth of its significance. Now, after much turbulence and many transitions, I bring my philosophy to life. Like all human explorations this is going to be turbulent maybe a little uncomfortable.

Souls of One's Feet is about what carries us when nothing else does - a lifelong invitation to hold hope; a vibration that has been at the heart of my musings for over two decades. For me an exploration on what it means to be human.

After much deliberation, observation and exploration, I have concluded that for me, being human is a journey of hope. Over time, I have mused in meanders mapping a poetic series that serve as a bridge to my philosophy. This bridge begins with The Timekeeper... although you may read any of my works in an order you choose...In remembrance that we all arrive in our own space - in time.

Throughout our human journey, we navigate endless avenues of emotion. We seek a middle ground - a harmonious balance - we never quite land in this space, not until we leave this earthly place.

What exactly are we searching for?

Why are we here?

What does it mean to be human?

There exists an empty space I refer to as the 'middle-way' . This is the space, where we pause. The space we feel between our humans experience. These pauses form, what I describe as sequences; sequences I map through my time.

In my observations, hope expands mostly in the sequences of joy. Rarely is it remarked upon in the quieter, more subtle sequences of discomfort. As human beings we dance through light and dark. Through the ebb and flow we call life, we are the dance of existence in time.

Each human experiences time that challenges them, a happening that changes the structure of reality. A loss, a trauma, a profound shift in how it feels to be human. These moments create ripples in frequencies that move through us. If they feel uncomfortable we may avoid-dance. We are always - dancing.

The purpose of these poetic explorations is to illuminate the sequences of hope and formulate a bridge to my life's work a philosophy that comes from my heart. To experience my musings in the hope that is intended I invite you to feel time and space in a way that may appear unusual, uncomfortable, or even uncertain. In this discomfort time expands. Uncertainty deepens our awareness of time, in these spaces we may examine layers of our existence through a lens of hope.

hope

INSPIRATION SURROUNDS US

Trees do not rush, yet they become rooted and firm. Their transformation is not loud — it is patient, elegant, eternal. They teach us what it means to grow without force, to reach without grasping, to change while remaining deeply connected to self. We are not separate we are made of the same earth, fed by the same light, moved by the same unseen winds. Inspiration surrounds us because it is us — unfolding leaf by leaf, season by season.

In every fallen branch, in every ring of age beneath the bark, there is a story of endurance, shedding, and renewal. The tree does not fear winter, nor cling to spring - it trusts the cycle, even in the stillness. So too do our lives spiral inward and outward, full of invisible turning points. We are walking forests, shedding old selves, rooting deeper even as we rise. Transformation is not a destination - it is the sacred rhythm of being alive. The sacred rhythm of breathing and beating. The sacred rhythm of hope.

This book is a gathering of such rhythms - poems shaped like branches, truths buried like roots. These verses are offerings to the wild within and the wild around us. In reading them, may you remember what the trees have always known: that to be alive is to be in constant becoming, and that every moment, no matter how small, is a seed of change waiting to bloom.

Read along with me on my poetry channel.
Let's journey together through the verses, allowing the words to resonate and unfold.

www.soulsofonesfeet.bandcamp.com

THE TREES ETERNAL FLOW

SOULS OF ONES FEET
A PHILOSOPHY OF HOPE

Transforming Trees is a poetic exploration of the subtle strength and quiet resilience of nature, seen through the lens of my heart in avenues of time, love, and hope. This journey takes you through twelve distinct flows - each one a exploration on the timeless presence of trees and the lessons they offer about endurance, transformation, connection and resilience. As the trees stand firm, their roots entwined with the earth, they remind us that even in moments of uncertainty and change, there is profound wisdom in simply being.

The inspiration for this exploration came unexpectedly, as I stood before a great tree, its branches reaching upward as if in silent conversation with the sky. There, in that stillness, I began to feel a quiet invitation - a call to observe, to listen, and to learn from the way nature finds strength in both its stillness and its motion.

The trees, ancient and wise, hold a secret that only those who pause may feel the spaces between. There are seasons of silence, of waiting, of unseen transformation, and in the midst of these, there is always movement.

This collection invites you to join me in observing these quiet giants. As we flow we are guided to feel the trees not only as symbols of nature's strength but as reflections of our own existence. I invite you to witness the pathways that open when we stop to observe and listen to the quiet rhythms of the world around us. Like the trees, we may stand resilient in the face of adversity, we may embrace the constant dance of change in acceptance that this is all part of being human.

In Transforming Trees, the question is not just about how the trees endure, but how we, too, can transform through the cycles and seasons of time, rooted in the earth and ever reaching for the light. Join me in this journey, and let the wisdom of the trees guide you through and to - your heart space.

What do the trees whisper, are we still enough to listen?
How do their ancient roots guide our human hope?

FLOW ONE

There is a dance
An eloquent elusive dance
In the memory of the roots
The avenues buried beneath
A sanctuary of space
A sap a serenity
A timeless patient grace

Nature gifts us many things
Through time our journey becomes clear
We transform like the trees in the wind
Always far but ever so near

A raw knowing awaits in an empty space
—Elusive race
Holding hope in motion as transformation it takes place

Breathe—hold a moment for you
Allow time to fall away
The trees transform so eloquently
— they show us everyday
When transformation aligns with timelessness
There resides a space to breathe
Love and hope bring harmony
Patience aids to heal

Nature gifts us many things
Through time our journey it becomes clear
We transform like the trees in the wind
Always far but ever so near

Time in motion rocks
 Transformation flows

As the middle way departs
Eloquent release
The sun descends and the moon it rises
As time does never cease
That's the way time goes
In the space that is awaiting
Did fear just creep in
The quiet space you chose
Like the unfolding of the petals
From a summer—spring— time— rose

The trees continue to guide us
Breathe in
— Now breathe out
Listen to your rhythm
Whenever there is doubt
Know the thread that falters through the leaves
Within the changing seasons
— that is when it's time to breathe

Hold space with universal nature
Through the transforming of the trees

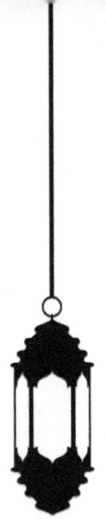

FLOW TWO

There is a dance
An eloquent elusive dance
That holds colours in varitian
As the light waves blend in oculus ways
An eloquent peaceful meander
Unraveled as time holds the rays

The trees continue to guide us
Breathe in—
 — Now breathe out
Listen to my rhythm
Whenever there is doubt
Nature gifts us many things
Through time our journey becomes clear
We transform like the trees in the wind
Always far but ever so near

The bark so brittle so tender
The earth beneath its feet
These delicate intrinsic pathways- hidden underneath

Yet, I can't quite fathom the time scale
Through a time maybe whence— maybe when
The universe gifted such detail
A beginning before time can tell
Now the motion meanders
A sequence I leave for you
Through these delicate eloquent pathways
A guide, an offering through
These turbulent trajectories
 Transforming beneath the trees
Dancing along the oceans
Capturing hope in a breeze

The trees transforms so delicately
They dance as they embrace the wind
Flowing in time gracefully
A heart held beneath the thick skin

The sun shines on the leaves
Reminding us with gentleness and ease
That heavens lay beneath
The transformation of these trees
Nature gifts us many things
Through time our journey becomes clear
We transform like the trees in the wind
Always far but ever so near
Let us listen
To the meanderance in motion
The meticulous occultation
The melody
The rhythm
Our time in its grandest rotation
It is we that transform the tapestry
It is we that set the pace
Let us hold hope in harmony
Let us hold love in this space
Let us hold a moment

Breathe in
 —Now breathe out

Observe these timeless avenues
Whenever you hold doubt
Acknowledge the space that falls between
The avenues of all time
As the trees gift us pathways
To gently realign

Time we may know
Not time we once knew
For the dance - is merely a meanderance
Through stages of hope held in you

FLOW THREE

Have we not been here before?
A beginning through a root
A sequence quite embedded
Aloof and underfoot
The Souls of One's Feet brings healing
When we connect through this space in time
There is a trajectory held within each of us
A core understanding divine

The trees continue transforming
Time gently passes—we patiently await
A season held in the masses
The gift - pure allurance
Is not some illusion hidden in rhyme
Merely a meander of motion
A transformed occupation
A tree held in its prime

There is this middle way
Where the sap gentle flows to a grace
Hearty
    Healthy
 Human
    Holding ground to a pace
Tic Toc - goes the rhythm
A bark, a willow
An oak
As we weave with wonderment
All that time does evoke
The trees continue to guide us
The trees continue to show
That time is merely miraculous
A gift - that continues to grow

The trees continue to guide us
Breathe in
— Now breathe out
Listen to your rhythm
Whenever there is doubt

FLOW FOUR

Grand beautiful fellow
I hear the the footsteps bellow
Clank
    Clonk
Clank
    Clonk
 Halt
Ambiguous—animosity
Deliverance to fault

There is this flow
An eloquent drift as the seasons shift
Leaves as they lift to the air
Gracing there way to the ground
Featherweight—fortifying—found

Nature gifts us many things
Through time our journey becomes clear
We transform like the trees in the wind
Always far—ever so near
Nature neatly arranges—the flow of time in its stages
Yet, not before dancing
Alluring enhancing—enchanting
The world as it spins in formation
Spirals and spins—fluctuations

There is this flow
An eloquent drift as the seasons shift
The leaves they lift to the air
As we inhale and we exhale
Observe and examine
The pause the drift and delay

We follow the flux
     We flow
 We uncover our meander—we grow

The oak stands to ground
To halt at the sound
When unsure which way one should go

FLOW FIVE

Listen to the crunch
The melodic distant hunch
As you step on a twig and it snaps
A reminder
A gentle delightful meander
As the forest invites and evokes
To follow the flux—we must flow
To uncover a meander—we grow

The oak stands to ground
To halt at the sound
When unsure which way one should go

A crossroads appear
The almond stands near
The apple an orchard encounter
The sap takes us back
To a middle aftermath
Where our blood it flows like a stream
A avenue laid open
The apple is hoping
The almond transforms into shades
Pinks, whites and featherlights
As the glow it radiates

Nature gifts us many things
Through time our journey becomes clear
We transform like the trees in the wind
Always far—ever so near

Time in motion rocks
 Transformation flows
As the middle way departs
 Eloquent release
The sun descents
      The moon it rises
As time does never cease
That's the way time goes
In the space that is awaiting
Did fear just creep in?
The quiet space you chose
Like the unfolding of the almond
Or the apple as it grows

These trees continue to guide us
Breathe in
 —Now breathe out
Listen to my rhythm
Whenever there is doubt
Know that time it passes
The flow it never ends
When we observe within formation
The way the oak—it wends

FLOW SIX

There is a place I cannot show you
A middleway before my time
A space I may only guide
In the hope that you feel to shine
For, it radiates within you
 Without it pulsates

Extremities
    Extremities
Anchor—then await

The passing in a moment
A rare palm that branches out
Casting rays in sunshine
 A midvien—a apex
No shadows—nor no doubt

A gentle reminder
  A peaceful meander
The flow is quite elusive
The skies are bright and blue
The palm trees
      The palm trees
The dance is slow and smooth

There is a dance
An eloquent elusive rhythm
Royalty and trailormaids
Catastrophe and serenades
The palm trees
      The palm trees
The browns

The greens
 The greys

The trees continue to guide us
The trees transform everyday
Patience
 Patience
Time will show the way

Nature gifts us many things
Through time our journey becomes clear
We transform like the trees in the wind
Always far—ever so near

FLOW SEVEN

There is a magnificence and magnitude to a mango
Not as slender as a maple
 Nor as pristine as the queen
A verdant testament to the abundance unforeseen
A mute embodiment of wisdom
A tree that transforms into spice
Sweet- flavoursome
Hesitant— as elegance
Whispers delight

There is a beauty in the canopy
A universal phase
That bellows in the sunshine
And echoes in the shade

The trees continues to guide us
If we listen they hold time in space
To gentle remind one to breathe
As we evolve—time opens the stage

Listen—feel in your heart the mango
Its serene presence and posture
That has anchored through resilience
Its cracks a mere contour
An avenue
     An opening

A middleway in time
     A mango
 A mango
So sweet as is divine
Gifting lightwaves
Lightwaves
A melody in time

A tree transforming tropically
The sun beats and beats for days
Then the battering of the rain storm
Still it glows in shades
Greens, yellows and purples
Orange and reds too
The mango
    The mango
Beauty through and through
Nature gifts us many things
When we observe—when we open our heart
We transform like the trees in the tropics
Grounded, joyful
 Gentle tonics

This is a gentle meanderance
A gift
A flow through nature
As a kisadee softly lands
A reminder of connections - not capture
Elegance
Fruitful
Patient—rooted firm
Weathering the seasons
The trees continue to guide
The mango
    The apple
The pear
Eloquent—graceful
Gratitude—our universe in full flare

FLOW EIGHT

There is an eternal cycle to the seasons
Where the trees gently guide—through feelings
In elegance—with grace
The trees transform so beautifully
No division—gently pace
The leaves fall through the avenues
Gifting persuasion of all sorts
As they are welcomed by mother earth
A renewal
A form of rebirth

There is a sanctity
In the sealing
When we observe in creation
These feelings
A dance between the seasons
A eloquent elusive dance
The pistachio
    The walnut
 The fig formulating trends
To gift us means to existence
To nurture as the physical depends
On the fruit—through the fabrics
 Intrinsic pathways that maverick
The pockets of peace that echoes and calls
 As father sky- gifts—rainfall
To gently shower these sacred sanctuaries
That eloquently decorate the halls

FLOW NINE

The trees continue to guide us
Through the anchors they gift and they Embellish
A sacred distinction
A midway—through a fraught jurisdiction
A highway

Our modern world
 Our modern world
Disregards the purpose at pace
Through removal—of natures true place
A space
 A spectacular unobserved race
The trees
 The trees
They whistle through the breeze- the trees

The magnificent magnolia
The mango, the mustard—the maple
The dragon that flowers each crown that its grown
A eloquently patience
A umbrella of love—gently sown

The trees continue to guide us
If we listen without judgment and fear
We may softly hear
 We may gently feel
The wisdom in the roots
The echoes through the cycles
That spin on a bark
As burl wood re-cycles

There is a sanctity
In the sealing
When we observe in creation
These feelings

FLOW TEN

A seed, an embryonic antibiotic
This is where hope begins
In a middleway where branches expand
As the wind does demand
The motion— dispersed into land

The trees continue to guide us
To gracefully show and to tell
If we listen through the airwaves
The oak
 Wood
 Stairways
The carpenter—an expert to hand
Of the gifts nature offers—In community and kind
Yet the sap falls
      as we puncture the rind
The soft and the hard
The texture that's scarred
From the axe and the chisel—we drove
The bellows
 The trees—tremendous echoes

> *"If you listen to my heartbeat*
> *If you observe the seasons flow*
> *You will know I am here to guide you*
> *In the way nature does flow*
> *When we are one with nature*
> *The mechanical will decrease*
> *We will feel hope most abundantly*
> *As patience collides with peace"*

FLOW ELEVEN

Nature gifts us many things
Through time our journey becomes clear
We transforms like the trees in the wind
Open your heart
        Embrace any fear

For, nature neatly arranges
The time as we know it in stages
If we only observe the trees dancing
Alluring—eloquently, enchanting

The trees sway to show
That even in the winter they shiver
The cold and extremes feel quite bitter
Retract
      Recoil
Recalibrate
The sun's glow will soon alleviate
The frosting and the freezing—of leaving

Observe the movement
The graceful stretch through the spring
Summer—shadowing
As Autumn tip toes in—
The trees are a miraculous marvel
Eras and years—they debarkle
The dioxides—the particles
On hillsides—and lakesides—and landslides-
The harmful to humans oxides
Our friend keeps us safe
 We survive

FLOW TWELVE

There are thousands of trees at our feet
Communicating ground deep
Through the roots
 Through the core
If we listen and open our heart
Where love and hope do depart

We may hear
    We may feel

That the trees continue to guide us
Aligned—almost surreal
An embryonic encounter
A seedling that arrived before time
These magnificent elders
Standing in their prime
The oak
 The willow—a juniper quite commonly found
There are trillions of trees on our earth
There home is a place in the ground
Anchored to their mother
As their father—the wind and the sky
Kisses them with raindrops
To nurture their space in your time

The trees continue to guide us
To gracefully show and to tell
If we listen through the airwaves
The oak
Wood
Stairways

**GRATITUDE & JOY
LIVE HERE**

SEASONS OF TIME

POETIC EXTENSION

As we draw to the close of this poetic journey through the trees and nature, I invite you to pause and reflect on the quiet rhythm that unites us all—the dance of time, ever flowing and ever changing.

In Seasons of Time, the flow of nature is mirrored in the passage of our own lives. Just as the trees shed their leaves in the autumn, so too do we experience moments of letting go. Just as the first buds of spring herald renewal, so too does each new cycle in our lives carry the promise of fresh beginnings.

This shorter flow invites you into an intimate space where time is a series of seasons—each one bringing its own wisdom. Reminding us that, like the trees, we are never stagnant; we are always in the process of becoming. The seasons unfold within us.

In the quiet of this exploration, you will find the invitation to recognise the patterns of time as they echo in nature. To consider how the passing of moments, much like the cycles of the earth, offers us a continuous opportunity to examine the space our time lives.

As you read, I invite you to look within—allow the words to stir something deep inside, reflect on your own journey through time. Just as the trees stand firm, rooted in their place yet ever responsive to the changing seasons, so too do we have the power to grow, evolve, and transform in harmony with the rhythms of the universe.

SEASONS OF TIME

Seasons into seasons
A timeless sequence
A grand— temporal experience

Here we are - Is your world as mine?
Or do you read my words through an alternative space in time?
Shall we flow back to the beginning to recap— to understand
The seasons are a gift
They formulate to show
If we are not at one with nature
                       Then one or both must go

Seasons of time are passing
Breathtaking avenues collapsing
Yet here we stand
Through digital demand
Our human race amassing
While the seasons continue passing

Spring into summer
a warming phase - a gift
to focus on the light
— That shines down from the heavens—a glorified delight
The flowers have emerged
The trees extend there branches
Seasons passing
      Humans flock in masses
The beaches — the paradise
—the space we long to be

Before autumn creeps the corridors
 - With darkness unforseen
Yet there is beauty in the middleway
 - In the space in time we hold
As we emerge within alignment of the hallways we have chose

The seasons continue to pass
 - the stories the stages don't last
A moment with meaning
A time held in feeling
The seasons
    These - seasons of being

Wherever you arrive in this moment to flow
—hold an open heart
Let in—as you let go

Allow the seasons to gently guide you
—to the endless extremities in time

As you meander through the corridors
—of a world which - you align

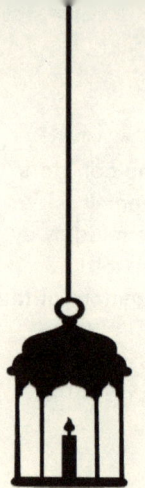

OTHER WORKS
BY AMY CECILIA GRAINGER

A Philosophy of Hope

The Space Time Lives In
Emerging Through Time and Space

Selected Poetry Collections
The Timekeeper
Houses of Hope
Transforming Trees
Chemistry

CONTINUING THE INQUIRY

HOW DOES IT FEEL TO BE HUMAN?

Thank you for spending time within these poems.

Transforming Trees forms part of a wider body of work exploring time, hope, and human existence through both poetry and philosophy. While these poems approach experience through image and rhythm, the philosophical works examine the same questions through sustained inquiry.

If the reflections within this collection resonate with you, the exploration continues in:

>The Space Time Lives In
>Book I of A Philosophy of Hope

With Love

Amy S

www.ingramcontent.com/pod-product-compliance
Lightning Source LLC
Chambersburg PA
CBHW020736020526
44118CB00033B/947